KT-579-146

POEMS OF HENRY LAWSON

Volume Two

SWEENEY II
Oil on hardboard 45 cm × 35 cm 1975

POEMS OF
HENRY LAWSON

Volume Two

Illustrated by Pro Hart

Ure Smith · Sydney

First published in 1975 by
Ure Smith Sydney
a division of Paul Hamlyn Pty Ltd
176 South Creek Rd, Dee Why West, Australia 2099

National Library of Australia Card
Number and ISBN 0 7254 0234 2
Photocomposed by Hartland & Hyde Filmsetting Pty Ltd
Printed in Hong Kong

2nd impression 1976
3rd impression 1978

Jacket painting: Corny Bill (detail)
Oil on hardboard 35 cm x 45 cm

Contents

"DEAD DUGGAN" FROM TALBRAGAR
Oil on hardboard 45 cm × 35 cm 1975

Introduction

Henry Lawson, 'The People's Poet', was born on the goldfields near Grenfell, New South Wales, on June 17, 1867. Soon after his birth, the Lawsons returned to Eurunderee where his father—Niels Hertzberg Larsen, anglicized to Peter Lawson—had previously taken up land.

Henry was already nine years old when a school ('The Old Bark School') opened at Eurunderee in 1876. About this time the deafness which was to plague him all his life became apparent. Before he turned fourteen he left school to help his father who had given up farming and was building houses in the district.

In 1883 his parents' marriage came to an end. His mother, Louisa, moved to Sydney, and Henry joined her there. Soon he was apprenticed as a coach-painter by Hudson Holdings at Clyde. Travelling to and from work he saw the poor living conditions in many of the slum areas. At home with Louisa, Lawson met many of the radicals of the day, and his ideals and his desire for social reform led him to try his hand at poetry.

In October 1887 Lawson had his first poem, 'Song of the Republic', published in its entirety in the *Bulletin*. In 1888 'Faces in the Street', a moving comment on the social injustice of the times, followed and Lawson became famous almost overnight. His reputation as a poet now established, he began also to work in the prose form. His first short story, 'His Father's Mate', was published in December, 1888. Lawson embarked on a journalistic career and travelled over much of Australia looking for work. He found that the freelance writer's lot is not an easy one. By 1892, despite his early success as a poet, Lawson was feeling dispirited and rejected, and his problem with alcohol was growing rapidly. Then J. F. Archibald, editor of the *Bulletin*, sent Lawson to Bourke in 1892–93 to report on the great drought. This trip provided Lawson with further material and insights for much of his writing especially that extolling the creed of mateship.

In 1894 Lawson helped his mother to print his first book, *Short Stories in Prose and Verse*, which was well received but was not a financial success. In 1895 he signed contracts with Angus and Robertson for two books, *In the Days When the World was Wide* and *While the Billy Boils*. Henry married Bertha Bredt in 1896. In an effort to escape from his alcohol problem they moved first to Western Australia and then to New Zealand, where his son James was born in 1898. Later that year the Lawsons returned to Sydney and Henry continued to write between drinking bouts. In 1900, shortly after the birth of his daughter, Bertha, Henry took his family to London to begin a new life.

At first he was successful; he was encouraged by the critics and had stories published in the leading journals. Eventually Henry started drinking heavily again and Bertha's health was unable to stand the strain. By the end of 1902 the Lawsons had returned to Sydney yet again. In 1903 Bertha separated from Henry. His decline began to gather momentum.

He continued to drink heavily and suffered a general deterioration of his health. Only occasionally did his writing echo the brilliance and spontaneity of his earlier work. For his income he was dependent on the generosity of his friends and a small literary pension from the Federal Government. Mrs Byers, whom he referred to as his 'little landlady', was his closest friend in his last years and he died at her cottage at Abbotsford on September 2, 1922. Henry Lawson was given a State funeral and buried in Waverley Cemetery.

Despite his personal problems, Henry Lawson is one of the few writers who has played a vital part in shaping the national identity of all Australians and moulding the Australian tradition. His poems have a dramatic simplicity that allowed him to reach the ordinary Australian. They were read and recited wherever the *Bulletin* carried his message. His poems of life in the city and the bush retain their vigour and continue to charm generations of Australians.

Grog-an'-Grumble Steeplechase

'Twixt the coastline and the border lay the town of
Grog-an'-Grumble
(Just two pubs beside a racecourse in a wilderness of sludge)
An' they say the local meeting was a drunken rough-and-tumble,
Which was ended pretty often by an inquest on the judge.
Yes, 'tis said the city talent very often caught a tartar
In the Grog-an'-Grumble sportsman, 'n' retired with
broken heads,
For the fortune, life, and safety of the Grog-an'-Grumble starter
Mostly hung upon the finish of the local thoroughbreds.

Pat M'Durmer was the owner of a horse they called The
Screamer,
Which he called the "quickest shtepper 'twixt the Darling
and the sea,"
But I think it's very doubtful if a Banshee-haunted dreamer
Ever saw a more outrageous piece of equine scenery;
For his points were most decided, from his end to his beginning;
He had eyes of different colour, and his legs they wasn't mates.
Pat M'Durmer said he always came "widin a flip av winnin',"
An' his sire had come from England, 'n' his dam was from the
States.

Friends would argue with M'Durmer, and they said he was in
error
To put up his horse The Screamer, for he'd lose in any case,
And they said a city racer by the name of Holy Terror
Was regarded as the winner of the coming steeplechase;
Pat declared he had the knowledge to come in when it was raining,
And irrelevantly mentioned that he knew the time of day,
So he rose in their opinion. It was noticed that the training
Of The Screamer was conducted in a dark, mysterious way.

Well, the day arrived in glory; 'twas a day of jubilation
For the careless-hearted bushmen quite a hundred miles
around,
An' the rum 'n' beer 'n' whisky came in waggons from the
station,
An' the Holy Terror talent were the first upon the ground.
Judge M'Ard—with whose opinion it was scarcely safe to
wrestle—
Took his dangerous position on the bark-and-sapling stand:
He was what the local Stiggins used to speak of as a "wessel
Of wrath," and he'd a bludgeon that he carried in his hand.

"Off ye go!" the starter shouted, as down fell a stupid jockey;
Off they started in disorder—left the jockey where he lay—
And they fell and rolled and galloped down the crooked course and rocky,
Till the pumping of The Screamer could be heard a mile away.
But he kept his legs and galloped; he was used to rugged courses,
And he lumbered down the gully till the ridge began to quake:
And he ploughed along the sidling, raising earth till other horses
An' their riders, too, were blinded by the dust-cloud in his wake.

From the ruck he'd struggle slowly—they were much surprised to find him
Close abeam of Holy Terror as along the flat they tore—
Even higher still and denser rose the cloud of dust behind him,
While in more divided splinters flew the shattered rails before.
"Terror!" "Dead heat!" they were shouting—"Terror!" but The Screamer hung out
Nose to nose with Holy Terror as across the creek they swung,
An' M'Durmer shouted loudly, "Put yer tongue out, put yer tongue out!"
An' The Screamer put his tongue out, and he won by half-a-tongue.

GROG-AN'-GRUMBLE STEEPLECHASE
Oil on hardboard 35 cm × 45 cm 1975

Here's Luck

Old Time is tramping close to-day—you hear his bluchers fall,
A mighty change is on the way, an' God protect us all;
Some dust'll fly from beery coats—at least it's been declared.
I'm glad that women has the votes—but just a trifle scared.

I'm just a trifle scared—For why? The women mean to rule;
I feel just like in days gone by when I was caned at school.
The days of men is nearly dead—of double moons and stars—
They'll soon put out our pipes, 'tis said, an' close the public bars.

No more we'll take a glass of ale to banish care an' strife,
An' chuckle home with that old tale we used to tell the wife.
We'll laugh an' joke an' sing no more with jolly beery chums,
Or shout "Here's luck!" while waitin' for the luck that never
comes.

Did we prohibit swillin' tea—clean out of commonsense!—
Or legislate 'gainst gossipin' across a backyard fence?
Did we prohibit bustles, or the hoops when they was here?
The women never think of this—yet want to stop our beer.

The track o' life is dry enough, an' crossed with many a rut,
But, oh! we'll find it rougher still when all the pubs is shut,
When all the pubs is shut, an' closed the doors we used to seek,
An' we go toilin', thirstin' on through Sundays all the week.

For since the days when pubs was "inns"—in years gone
past 'n' far—
Poor sinful souls have drowned their sins an' sorrows at the bar;
An' though at times it led to crime, an' debt, and such
complaints—
Will times be happier in the days when all mankind is saints?

'Twould make the bones of Bacchus leap an' bust his coffin lid;
And Burns' ghost would wail an' weep as Robbie never did;
But let the preachers preach in style, an' rave, and rant, 'n' buck,
I rather guess they'll hear awhile the old war-cry;
"Here's Luck!"

The world may wobble round the sun, an' all the banks go bung,
But pipes'll smoke, an' liquor run, while *Auld Lang Syne*
is sung.
While men are driven through the mill, an' flinty times is struck,
They'll find the private entrance still!
Here's Luck, old man—Here's Luck!

HERE'S LUCK
Oil on hardboard 35 cm × 45 cm 1975

Corny Bill

His old clay pipe stuck in his mouth,
  His hat pushed from his brow,
His dress best fitted for the South—
  I think I see him now;
And when the streets are very still,
  And sleep upon me comes,
I often dream that me an' Bill
  Are humpin' of our drums.

I mind the time when first I came
  A stranger to the land;
And I was stumped, an' sick, an' lame
  When Bill took me in hand.
And when we'd journeyed damp an' far,
  An' clouds were in the skies,
We'd camp in some old shanty bar,
  And sit a-tellin' lies.

Though time had writ upon his brow
  And rubbed away his curls,
He always was—an' may be now—
  A favourite with the girls;
I've heard bush-wimmin scream an' squall—
  I've see'd 'em laugh until
They could not do their work at all,
  Because of Corny Bill.

He was the jolliest old pup
  As ever you did see,
And often at some bush kick-up
  They'd make old Bill M.C.
He'd make them dance and sing all night,
  He'd make the music hum,
But he'd be gone at mornin' light
  A-humpin' of his drum.

Though joys of which the poet rhymes
  Was not for Bill an' me,
I think we had some good old times
  Out on the wallaby.
I took a wife and left off rum,
  An' camped beneath a roof;
But Bill preferred to hump his drum
  A-paddin' of the hoof.

"THE DREAM" FROM CORNY BILL
Oil on hardboard 35 cm × 45 cm 1975

The lazy, idle loafers wot
   In toney houses camp
Would call old Bill a drunken sot,
   A loafer, or a tramp;
But if the dead get up again—
   As preachers say they will—
I'd take my chance of judgment then
   Along of Corny Bill.

His long life's day is nearly o'er,
   Its shades begin to fall;
He soon must sling his bluey for
   The last long tramp of all;
I trust that when, in bush an' town,
   He's lived and laughed his fill,
They'll let the golden sliprails down
   For poor old Corny Bill.

CORNY BILL
Oil on hardboard 35 cm × 45 cm 1975

CUTTING CANEGRASS
Oil on hardboard 35 cm × 45 cm 1975

Paroo River

It was a week from Christmas-time,
  As near as I remember,
And half a year since, in the rear,
  We'd left the Darling Timber.
The track was hot and more than drear;
  The day dragged out for ever;
But now we knew that we were near
  Our Camp—the Paroo River.

With blighted eyes and blistered feet,
  With stomachs out of order,
Half-mad with flies and dust and heat
  We'd crossed the Queensland Border.
I longed to hear a stream go by
  And see the circles quiver;
I longed to lay me down and die
  That night on Paroo River.

The "nose-bags" heavy on each chest
  (God bless one kindly squatter!),
With grateful weight our hearts they
  pressed—
  We only wanted water.
The sun was setting in a spray
  Of colour like a liver—
We'd fondly hoped to camp and stay
  That night by Paroo River.

A cloud was on my mate's broad brow,
  And once I heard him mutter:
"What price the good old Darling, now?—
  God bless that grand old gutter!"
And then he stopped and slowly said
  In tones that made me shiver:
"It cannot well be on ahead—
  I think we've crossed the river."

But soon we saw a strip of ground
  Beside the track we followed,
No damper than the surface round,
  But just a little hollowed.
His brow assumed a thoughtful frown—
  This speech he did deliver:
"I wonder if we'd best go down
  Or up the blessed river?"

"But where," said I, " 's the blooming stream?"
  And he replied, "We're at it!"
I stood awhile, as in a dream,
  "Great Scott!" I cried, "is *that* it?
Why, that is some old bridle-track!"
  He chuckled, "Well, I never!
It's plain you've never been Out Back—
  This *is* the Paroo River!"

NEAR THE DARLING RIVER
Oil on hardboard 35 cm × 45 cm 1975

Knocking Around

Weary old wife, with the bucket and cow,
"How's your son Jack? and where is he now?"
Haggard old eyes that turn to the west—
"Boys will be boys, and he's gone with the rest!"
Grief without tears and grief without sound;
"Somewhere up-country he's knocking around."
   Knocking around with a vagabond crew,
   Does for himself what a mother would do;
   Maybe in trouble and maybe hard-up,
   Maybe in want of a bite or a sup;
   Dead of the fever, or lost in the drought,
   Lonely old mother! he's knocking about.

Wiry old man at the tail of the plough,
"Heard of Jack lately? and where is he now?"
Pauses a moment his forehead to wipe,
Drops the rope reins while he feels for his pipe,
Scratches his grey head in sorrow or doubt:
"Somewhere or other he's knocking about."
   Knocking about on the runs of the West,
   Holding his own with the worst and the best,
   Breaking in horses and risking his neck,
   Droving or shearing and making a cheque;
   Straight as a sapling—six-foot, and sound,
   Jack is all right when he's knocking around.

KNOCKING AROUND
Oil on hardboard 45 cm × 35 cm 1975

OUT BACK I Oil on hardboard 27 cm × 71 cm 1975

Out Back

The old year went, and the new returned, in the withering weeks
of drought;
The cheque was spent that the shearer earned, and the sheds
were all cut out;
The publican's words were short and few, and the publican's
looks were black—
And the time had come, as the shearer knew, to carry his swag
Out Back.

For time means tucker, and tramp you must, where the scrubs and plains are wide,
With seldom a track that a man can trust, or a mountain peak to guide;
All day long in the dust and heat—when summer is on the track—
With stinted stomachs and blistered feet, they carry their swags Out Back.

He tramped away from the shanty there, when the days were
long and hot,
With never a soul to know or care if he died on the track or
not.
The poor of the city have friends in woe, no matter how much
they lack,
But only God and the swagman know how a poor man fares
Out Back.

He begged his way on the parched Paroo and the Warrego
tracks once more,
And lived like a dog, as the swagmen do, till the Western
stations shore;
But men were many, and sheds were full, for work in the
town was slack—
The traveller never got hands in wool, though he tramped for
a year Out Back.

In stifling noons when his back was wrung by its load, and the
air seemed dead,
And the water warmed in the bag that hung to his aching arm
like lead.
Or in times of flood, when plains were seas and the scrubs were
cold and black,
He ploughed in mud to his trembling knees, and paid for his
sins Out Back.

And dirty and careless and old he wore, as his lamp of hope
grew dim;
He tramped for years, till the swag he bore seemed part of
himself to him.
As a bullock drags in the sandy ruts, he followed the dreary
track,
With never a thought but to reach the huts when the sun went
down Out Back.

It chanced one day when the north wind blew in his face like a
furnace-breath.
He left the track for a tank he knew—'twas a shorter cut to
death;
For the bed of the tank was hard and dry, and crossed with
many a crack.
And, oh! it's a terrible thing to die of thirst in the scrub
Out Back.

A drover came, but the fringe of law was eastward many a mile:
He never reported the thing he saw, for it was not worth
his while.

OUT BACK II Oil on hardboard 35 cm × 45 cm 1975

The tanks are full, and the grass is high in the mulga off
the track,
Where the bleaching bones of a white man lie by his mouldering
swag Out Back.

For time means tucker, and tramp they must, where the plains
and scrubs are wide,
With seldom a track that a man can trust, or a mountain peak
to guide;
All day long in the flies and heat the men of the outside
track,
With stinted stomachs and blistered feet, must carry their swags
Out Back.

The Fire at Ross's Farm

The squatter saw his pastures wide
Decrease, as one by one
The farmers moving to the west
Selected on his run;
Selectors took the water up
And all the black-soil round;
The best grass-land the squatter had
Was spoilt by Ross's ground.

Now many schemes to shift old Ross
Had racked the squatter's brains,
But Sandy had the stubborn blood
Of Scotland in his veins;
He held the land and fenced it in,
He cleared and ploughed the soil,
And year by year a richer crop
Repaid him for his toil.

Between the homes for many years
The devil left his tracks:
The squatter 'pounded Ross's stock,
And Sandy 'pounded Black's.
A well upon the lower run
Was filled with earth and logs,
And Black laid baits about the farm
To poison Ross's dogs.

It was, indeed, a deadly feud
Of class and creed and race,
So Fate supplied a Romeo
And a Juliet in the case;
And more than once across the flats,
Beneath the Southern Cross,
Young Robert Black was seen to ride
With pretty Jenny Ross.

One Christmas time, when months of drought
Had parched the western creeks,
The bush-fires started in the north
And travelled south for weeks.
At night along the river-side
The scene was grand and strange—
The hill-fires looked like lighted streets
Of cities in the range.

THE FIRE AT ROSS'S FARM I
Oil on hardboard 45 cm × 35 cm 1975

The cattle-tracks between the trees
   Were like long dusky aisles,
And on a sudden breeze the fire
   Would sweep along for miles;
Like sounds of distant musketry
   It crackled through the brakes,
And o'er the flat of silver grass
   It hissed like angry snakes.

It leapt across the flowing streams
   And raced the pastures through;
It climbed the trees, and lit the boughs,
   And fierce and fiercer grew.
The bees fell stifled in the smoke
   Or perished in their hives,
And with the stock the kangaroos
   Went flying for their lives.

The sun had set on Christmas Eve,
   When through the scrub-lands wide
Young Robert Black came riding home
   As only natives ride.
He galloped to the homestead door
   And gave the first alarm:
"The fire is past the granite spur,
   And close to Ross's farm.

"Now, father, send the men at once,
   They won't be wanted here;
Poor Ross's wheat is all he has
   To pull him through the year."
"Then let it burn," the squatter said;
   "I'd like to see it done—
I'd bless the fire if it would clear
   Selectors from the run.

"Go if you will," the squatter said,
   "You shall not take the men—
Go out and join your precious friends,
   But don't come here again."
"I won't come back," young Robert cried,
   And, reckless in his ire,
He sharply turned his horse's head
   And galloped towards the fire.

THE FIRE AT ROSS'S FARM II
Oil on hardboard 35 cm × 45 cm 1975

And there for three long weary hours,
  Half-blind with smoke and heat,
Old Ross and Robert fought the flames
  That neared the ripened wheat.
The farmer's hand was nerved by fear
  Of danger and of loss;
And Robert fought the stubborn foe
  For love of Jenny Ross.

But serpent-like the curves and lines
  Slipped past them, and between
Until they reached the boundary where
  The old coach-road had been.
"The track is now our only hope,
  There we must stand," cried Ross,
"For nought on earth can stop the fire
  If once it gets across."

Then came a cruel gust of wind,
  And, with a fiendish rush,
The flames leapt o'er the narrow path
  And lit the fence of brush.
"The crop must burn!" the farmer cried,
  "We cannot save it now,"
And down upon the blackened ground
  He dashed his ragged bough.

But wildly, in a rush of hope,
  His heart began to beat,
For o'er the crackling fire he heard
  The sound of horses' feet.
"Here's help at last," young Robert cried,
  And even as he spoke
The squatter with a dozen men
  Came racing through the smoke.

Down on the ground the stockmen jumped
  And bared each brawny arm;
They tore green branches from the trees
  And fought for Ross's farm;
And when before the gallant band
  The beaten flames gave way,
Two grimy hands in friendship joined—
  And it was Christmas Day.

The Shanty on the Rise

When the caravans of wool-teams climbed the ranges from
the West,
On a spur among the mountains stood The Bullock-drivers'
Rest;
It was built of bark and saplings, and was rather rough
inside,
But 'twas good enough for bushmen in the careless days
that died—
Just a quiet little shanty kept by "Something-in-Disguise,"
As the bushmen called the landlord of the Shanty on the Rise.

City swells who "do the Royal" would have called the
Shanty low,
But 'twas better far and cleaner than some toney pubs
we know;
For the patrons of the Shanty had the principles of men,
And the spieler, if he struck it, wasn't welcome there again.
You could smoke and drink in quiet, yarn (or p'raps
soliloquize)
With a decent lot of fellows in the Shanty on the Rise.

'Twas the bullock-driver's haven when his team was on
the road,
And the waggon-wheels were groaning as they ploughed
beneath the load;
I remember how the teamsters struggled on while it was light,
Just to camp within a cooee of the Shanty for the night;
And I think the very bullocks raised their heads and fixed
their eyes
On the candle in the window of the Shanty on the Rise.

And the bullock-bells were clanking from the marshes on
the flats
As we hurried to the Shanty, where we hung our dripping
hats;
Then we took a drop of something that was brought at our
desire,
As we stood with steaming moleskins in the kitchen by the
fire.
Oh, it roared upon a fireplace of the good old-fashioned size,
When the rain came down the chimney of the Shanty on
the Rise.

They got up a Christmas party in the Shanty long ago,
While we camped with Jimmy Nowlett on the river-bank below;
Poor old Jim was in his glory—they'd elected him M.C.,
For there wasn't such another raving lunatic as he.
"Mr Nowlett! Mr Swaller!" shouted Something-in-Disguise,
As we walked into the parlour of the Shanty on the Rise.

There is little real pleasure in the city where I am—
There's a "swarry" round the corner with its mockery and
sham;
But a fellow can be happy when around the room he whirls
In a party Up-the-Country with the jolly country girls.
Why, at times I almost fancied I was dancing on the skies,
When I danced with Mary Carey in the Shanty on the Rise.

Jimmy came to me and whispered, and I muttered, "Go along!"
But he shouted "Mr Swaller will oblige us with a song!"
And at first I said I wouldn't, and I shammed a little too,
Till the girls began to whisper, "Mr Swallow, now, ah, *do!*"
So I sang a song of something 'bout the love that never dies,
And the chorus shook the rafters of the Shanty on the Rise.

Jimmy burst his concertina, and the bullock-drivers went
For the corpse of Joe the Fiddler, who was sleeping in his tent;
Joe was tired and had lumbago, and he wouldn't come, he said,
But the case was very urgent, so they pulled him out of bed;
And they fetched him, for the Bushmen knew that
Something-in-Disguise
Had a cure for Joe's lumbago in the Shanty on the Rise.

Jim and I were rather quiet while escorting Mary home,
'Neath the stars that hung in clusters, near and distant,
from the dome;
And we walked in such a silence, being lost in reverie,
That we heard the "settlers'-matches" softly rustle on the tree;
And I wondered who would win her, when she said her
sweet good-byes—
But she died at one-and-twenty, and was buried on the Rise.

I suppose the Shanty vanished from the ranges long ago,
And the girls are mostly married to the chaps I used to know.
My old chums are in the distance—some have crossed the
border-line,
But in fancy still their glasses chink against the rim of mine;
And, upon the very centre of the greenest spot that lies
In my fondest recollection, stands the Shanty on the Rise.

THE SHANTY ON THE RISE
Oil on hardboard 35 cm × 45 cm 1975

THE SONG AND THE SIGH Oil on hardboard 35 cm × 45 cm 1975

The Song and the Sigh

The creek went down with a broken song,
'Neath the sheoaks high;
The waters carried the tune along,
And the oaks a sigh.

The song and the sigh went winding by,
Went winding down;
Circling the foot of the mountain high
And the hillside brown.

They were hushed in the swamp of the Dead Man's Crime,
Where the curlews cried;
But they reached the river the selfsame time,
And there they died.

And the creek of life goes winding on,
Wandering by;
And bears for ever, its course upon,
A song and a sigh.

The Bush Fire

On the runs to the west of the Dingo Scrub there was drought,
and ruin, and death,
And the sandstorm came from the dread north-east with the
blast of a furnace-breath;
Till at last one day, at the fierce sunrise, a boundary-rider woke,
And saw in the place of the distant haze a curtain of light-blue
smoke.

There is saddling-up by the cocky's hut, and out in the
station yard,
And away to the north, north-east, north-west, the bushmen
are riding hard.
The pickets are out, and many a scout, and many a mulga wire,
While Bill and Jim, their faces grim, are riding to meet the fire.

It roars for days in the trackless scrub, and across, where the
ground seems clear,
With a crackle and rush, like the hissing of snakes, the fire
draws near and near;
Till at last, exhausted by sleeplessness, and the terrible toil and
heat,
The squatter is crying, "My God! the wool!" and the farmer,
"My God! the wheat!"

But there comes a drunkard (who reels as he rides) with news
from the roadside pub:—
"Pat Murphy—the cocky—cut off by the fire!—way back in
the Dingo Scrub!
Let the wheat and the woolshed go to ——" Well, they do as
each great heart bids;
They are riding a race for the Dingo Scrub—for Pat and his
wife and kids.

And who are leading the race with Death? An ill-matched three,
you'll allow;
Flash Jim the breaker and Boozing Bill (who is riding steadily
now),
And Constable Dunn, of the Mounted Police, on the grey
between the two
(He wants Flash Jim, but that job can wait till they get the
Murphys through).

As they strike the track through the blazing scrub, the trooper is
heard to shout:
"We'll take them on to the Two-mile Tank, if we cannot bring
them out!"
A half-mile more, and the rest rein back, retreating,
half-choked, half-blind;
And the three are gone from the sight of men, and the bush fire
roars behind.

The Bushmen wiped the smoke-made tears, and like Bushmen
laughed and swore.
"Poor Bill will be wanting his drink to-night as never he did
before."
"And Dunn was the best in the whole damned force!"
says a client of Dunn's, with pride;
"I reckon he'll serve his summons on Jim—when they get to the
other side."

. . . . . .

It is daylight again, and the fire is past, and the black scrub
silent and grim
Except for the blaze in an old dead tree, or the crash of a falling
limb;
And the Bushmen are riding across the waste, with hearts and
with eyes that fill,
To look at the bodies of Constable Dunn, Flash Jim, and
Boozing Bill.

They are found in the mud of the Two-mile Tank, where a fiend
might scarce survive,
But the Bushmen gather from words they hear that the bodies
are much alive.
There is Swearing Pat, with his grey beard singed, and language
of lurid hue,
And his tough old wife, and his half-baked kids, and the three
who dragged them through.

THE BUSH FIRE I
Oil on hardboard 35 cm × 45 cm 1975

THE BUSH FIRE II Oil on hardboard 27 cm × 71 cm 1975

Old Pat is deploring his burnt-out home, and his wife the
climate warm;
And Jim the loss of his favourite horse and Dunn of his
uniform;
And Boozing Bill, with a raging thirst, is cursing the Dingo
Scrub,
But all he'll ask is the loan of a flask and a lift to the nearest pub.

Flash Jim the Breaker is lying low—blue-paper is after Jim,
But Dunn, the trooper, is riding his rounds with a blind eye out
for him;
And Boozing Bill is fighting D.Ts. in the township of
Sudden Jerk—
When they're wanted again in the Dingo Scrub, they'll be there
to do the work.

Talbragar

Jack Denver died on Talbragar when Christmas Eve began,
And there was sorrow round the place, for Denver was a man;
Jack Denver's wife bowed down her head—her daughter's
grief was wild,
And big Ben Duggan by the bed stood sobbing like a child.
But big Ben Duggan saddled up, and galloped fast and far,
To raise the biggest funeral yet seen on Talbragar.
By station home
And shearing shed
Ben Duggan cried, "Jack Denver's dead!
Roll up at Talbragar!"

He borrowed horses here and there, and rode all Christmas Eve,
And scarcely paused a moment's time the mournful news to
leave;
He rode by lonely huts and farms until the day was done.
And then he turned his horse's head and made for Ross's Run.
No bushman in a single day had ridden half so far
Since Johnson brought the doctor to his wife at Talbragar.
By digger's camps
Ben Duggan sped—
At each he cried, "Jack Denver's dead!
Roll up at Talbragar!"

That night he passed the humpies of the splitters on the ridge,
And roused the bullock-drivers camped at Belinfante's Bridge;
And as he climbed the ridge again the moon shone on the rise—
Did moonbeams glisten in the mist of tears that filled his eyes?
He dashed the rebel drops away—for blinding things they are—
But 'twas his best and truest friend who died on Talbragar.
At Blackman's Run
Before the dawn,
Ben Duggan cried, "Jack Denver's gone!
Roll up at Talbragar!"

At all the shanties round the place they heard his horse's tramp,
He took the track to Wilson's Luck, and told the digger's camp;
But in the gorge by Deadman's Gap the mountain shades were
black,
And there a newly-fallen tree was lying on the track;
He saw too late—and then he heard the swift hoof's sudden jar,
And big Ben Duggan ne'er again rode home to Talbragar.
"The wretch is drunk,
And Denver's dead—
A burning shame!" the people said
Next day at Talbragar.

TALBRAGAR
Oil on hardboard 35 cm × 45 cm 1975

For thirty miles round Talbragar the boys rolled up in strength,
And Denver had a funeral a good long mile in length;
Round Denver's grave that Christmas Day rough Bushmen's
    eyes were dim—
The Western Bushmen knew the way to bury dead like him;
But some returning homeward found, by light of moon and star,
Ben Duggan lying in the rocks, five miles from Talbragar.

        And far and wide
        When Duggan died,
        The bushmen of the western side
        Rode in to Talbragar.

"DEAD DUGGAN" FROM TALBRAGAR
Oil on hardboard 45 cm × 35 cm 1975

The Old Bark School

It was built of bark and poles, and the roof was full of holes
And each leak in rainy weather made a pool;
And the walls were mostly cracks lined with calico and sacks—
There was little need for windows in the school.

Then we rode to school and back by the rugged gully-track,
On the old grey horse that carried three or four;
And he looked so very wise that he lit the Master's eyes
Every time he put his head in at the door.

(He had run with Cobb and Co.—"That grey leader, let him go!"
There were men "as knowed the brand upon his hide,"
Some "as knowed him on the course"—Funeral service:
"Good old horse!"
When we burnt him in the gully where he died.)

Kevin was the master's name, 'twas from Ireland that he came,
Where the tanks are always full, and feed is grand;
And the joker then in vogue said his lessons wid a brogue—
'Twas unconscious imitation, understand.

And we learnt the world in scraps from some ancient
dingy maps
Long discarded by the public-schools in town;
And as nearly every book dated back to Captain Cook
Our geography was somewhat upside-down.

It was "in the book" and so—well, at that we'd let it go,
For we never would believe that print could lie;
And we all learnt pretty soon that when school came out at noon
"The sun is in the south part of the sky."

And Ireland!—*that* was known from the coast-line to Athlone,
But little of the land that grave us birth;
Save that Captain Cook was killed (and was very likely grilled)
And "our blacks are just the lowest race on earth."

And a woodcut, in its place, of the same degraded race,
More like camels than the blackmen that we knew;
Jimmy Bullock, with the rest, scratched his head and gave it best;
But he couldn't stick a bobtailed kangaroo!

Now the old bark school is gone, and the spot it stood upon
Is a cattle-camp where curlews' cries are heard;
There's a brick school on the flat—an old schoolmate
teaches that—
It was built when Mr Kevin was "transferred."

THE OLD BARK SCHOOL I
Oil on hardboard 35 cm × 45 cm 1975

But the old school comes again with exchanges 'cross the plain—
With the *Out-Back Press* my fancy roams at large
When I read of passing stock, of a western mob or flock,
With James Bullock, Grey, or Henry Dale in charge.

When I think how Jimmy went from the old bark school content,
"Eddicated," with his packhorse after him,
Well . . . perhaps, if I were back, I would follow in his track,
And let Kevin "finish" me as he did Jim.

THE OLD BARK SCHOOL II
Oil on hardboard 35 cm × 45 cm 1975

The Old Jimmy Woodser

The old Jimmy Woodser comes into the bar
  Unwelcomed, unnoticed, unknown,
Too old and too odd to be drunk with, by far;
So he glides to the end where the lunch-baskets are
  And they say that he tipples alone.

His frockcoat is green and the nap is no more,
  And his hat is not quite at its best;
He wears the peaked collar our grandfathers wore,
The black-ribbon tie that was legal of yore,
  And the coat buttoned over his breast.

When first he came in, for a moment I thought
  That my vision or wits were astray;
For a picture and page out of Dickens he brought—
'Twas an old file dropped in from the Chancery Court
  To the wine-vault just over the way.

But I dreamed, as he tasted his "bitter" to-night
  And the lights in the bar-room grew dim,
That the shades of the friends of that other day's light,
And of girls that were bright in our grandfathers' sight.
  Lifted shadowy glasses to him.

Then I opened the door, and the old man passed out,
  With his short, shuffling step and bowed head;
And I sighed; for I felt, as I turned me about,
An odd sense of respect—born of whisky no doubt—
  For the life that was fifty years dead.

And I thought—there are times when our memory trends
  Through the future, as 'twere, on its own—
That I, out-of-date ere my pilgrimage ends,
In a new-fashioned bar to dead loves and dead friends
  Might drink, like the old man, alone.

THE OLD JIMMY WOODSER
Oil on hardboard 35 cm × 45 cm 1975

Sweeney

It was somewhere in September, and the sun was going down,
When I came, in search of copy, to a Darling-River town;
"Come-and-Have-a-Drink" we'll call it—'tis a fitting name,
I think—
And 'twas raining, for a wonder, up at Come-and-Have-a-Drink.

Underneath the pub veranda I was resting on a bunk
When a stranger rose before me, and he said that he was drunk;
He apologized for speaking; there was no offence, he swore;
But he somehow seemed to fancy that he'd seen my face before.

"No erfence," he said. I told him that he needn't mention it,
For I might have met him somewhere; I had travelled round a bit,
And I knew a lot of fellows in the Bush and in the streets—
But a fellow can't remember all the fellows that he meets.

Very old and thin and dirty were the garments that he wore,
Just a shirt and pair of trousers, and a boot, and nothing more;
He was wringing-wet and really in a sad and sinful plight,
And his hat was in his left hand, and a bottle in his right.

He agreed: You can't remember all the chaps you chance to meet,
And he said his name was Sweeney—people lived in Sussex-street.
He was camping in a stable, but he swore that he was right,
"Only for the blanky horses walkin' over him all night."

He'd apparently been fighting, for his face was black-and-blue,
And he looked as though the horses had been treading
on him, too;
But an honest, genial twinkle in the eye that wasn't hurt
Seemed to hint of something better, spite of drink
and rags and dirt.

It appeared that he mistook me for a long-lost mate of his—
One of whom I was the image, both in figure and in phiz—
(He'd have had a letter from him if the chap was livin' still,
For they'd carried swags together from the Gulf to Broken Hill).

Sweeney yarned awhile, and hinted that his folks were doing well,
And he told me that his father kept the Southern Cross Hotel;
And I wondered if his absence was regarded as a loss
When he left the elder Sweeney—landlord of the Southern Cross.

He was born in Parramatta, and he said, with humour grim,
That he'd like to see the city ere the liquor finished him,
But he couldn't raise the money. He was damned if he could think
What the Government was doing. Here he offered me a drink.

SWEENEY I
Oil on hardboard 35 cm × 45 cm 1975

I declined—'*twas* self-denial—and I lectured him on booze,
Using all the hackneyed arguments that preachers mostly use;
Things I'd heard in temperance lectures (I was young and
rather green),
And I ended by referring to the man he might have been.

Then a wise expression struggled with the bruises on his face,
Though his argument had scarcely any bearing on the case:
"What's the good o' keepin' sober? Fellers rise and fellers fall;
What I might have been and wasn't doesn't trouble me at all."

But he couldn't stay to argue, for his beer was nearly gone.
He was glad, he said, to meet me, and he'd see me later on,
But he guessed he'd have to go and get his bottle filled again;
And he gave a lurch and vanished in the darkness and the rain.

. . . . . .

And of afternoons in cities, when the rain is on the land,
Visions come to me of Sweeney with his bottle in his hand,
With the stormy night behind him, and the pub veranda-post—
And I wonder why he haunts me more than any other ghost.

I suppose he's tramping somewhere where the bushmen
carry swags,
Dragging round the western stations with his empty tucker-bags;
And I fancy that of evenings, when the track is growing dim,
What he "might have been and wasn't" comes along and
troubles him.

SWEENEY II
Oil on hardboard 45 cm × 35 cm 1975

Andy's Return

With pannikins all rusty,
   And billy burnt and black,
And clothes all torn and dusty
   That scarcely hide his back;
With sun-cracked saddle-leather,
   And knotted green-hide rein,
His face burnt brown with weather,
   Our Andy's home again!

His unkempt hair is faded
   With sleeping in the wet,
He's looking old and jaded;
   But he is hearty yet.
With eyes sunk in their sockets—
   But merry as of yore;
With big cheques in his pockets,
   Our Andy's home once more!

Old Uncle's bright and cheerful;
   He wears a smiling face;
And Aunty's never tearful
   Now Andy's round the place.
Old Blucher barks for gladness;
   He broke his rusty chain,
And leapt in joyous madness
   When Andy came again.

With tales of flood and famine
   On distant northern tracks,
And shady yarns—"baal gammon!"
   Of dealings with the blacks,
From where the skies hang lazy
   On many a northern plain,
From regions dim and hazy
   Our Andy's home again!

His toil is nearly over;
   He'll soon enjoy his gains.
No more he'll be a drover,
   And cross the lonely plains.
Where sheoaks bend and quiver
   Far from the hot North-west,
At home by some cool river
   He means to build our nest.

ANDY'S RETURN
Oil on hardboard 35 cm × 45 cm 1975

Hawkers

Dust, dust, dust and a dog—
   Oh, the sheep-dog won't be last,
Where the long, long shadow of the old bay horse
   With the shadow of his mate is cast.
A brick-brown woman, with her brick-brown kids,
   And a man with his head half-mast,
The feed-bags hung, and the bedding slung,
   And the blackened bucket made fast
Where the tailboard clings to the tucker and things—
   So the hawker's van goes past.

HAWKERS
Oil on hardboard 35 cm × 45 cm 1975

Ballad of Mabel Clare

Ye children of the Land of Gold,
   I sing this song to you,
And if the jokes are somewhat old
   The central facts are new.
So be it sung, by hut and tent,
   Where tall the native grows;
And understand, the song is meant
   For singing through the nose.

There dwelt a hard old cockatoo
   On western hills far out,
Where everything is green and blue
   (Except, of course, in drought);
A crimson Anarchist was he—
   Held other men in scorn—
Yet preached that every man is free,
   And also "ekal born."

He lived in his ancestral hut—
   His missus wasn't there—
There was none other with him but
   His daughter, Mabel Clare.
Her eyes and hair were like the sun;
   Her foot was like a mat;
Her cheeks a trifle overdone;
   She was a democrat.

A manly independence, born
   Among the hills, she had;
She treated womankind with scorn,
   And often cursed her dad.
She hated swells and shining lights,
   For she had seen a few,
And she believed in Women's Rights
   (She mostly got 'em, too).

A stranger on the neighbouring run
   Sojourned, the squatter's guest;
He was unknown to anyone,
   But exquisitely dress'd;
He wore the latest toggery,
   The loudest thing in ties—
'Twas generally reckoned he
   Was something in disguise.

BALLAD OF MABEL CLARE I Oil on hardboard 45 cm × 35 cm 1975

Once strolling in the noontide heat
  Beneath the blinding glare,
This noble stranger chanced to meet
  The radiant Mabel Clare.
She saw at once he was a swell—
  According to her lights—
But, ah! 'tis very sad to tell,
  She met him oft of nights.

And, rambling through the moonlit gorge,
   She chatted all the while
Of Ingersoll, and Henry George,
   And Bradlaugh and Carlyle:
In short, he learned to love the girl,
   And things went on like this,
Until he said he was an Earl,
   And asked her to be his.

"Oh, say no more, Lord Kawlinee,
   Oh, say no more!" she said;
"Oh, say no more, Lord Kawlinee,
   I wish that I was dead:
My head is in an awful whirl,
   The truth I dare not tell—
I am a democratic girl,
   And cannot wed a swell!"

"O Love!" he cried, "but you forget
   That you are most unjust;
'Twas not my fault that I was set
   Within the upper crust.
Heed not the yarns the poets tell—
   O Darling, do not doubt
A simple lord can love as well
   As any rouseabout!

"For you I'll give my fortune up—
   I'd go to work for you!
I'll put the money in the cup
   And drop the title, too.
Oh, fly with me! Oh, fly with me
   Across the mountains blue!
Hoh, fly with me! *Hoh, fly with me!*"
   That very night she flew.

They took the train and journeyed down;
   Across the range they sped
Until they came to Sydney town,
   Where shortly they were wed.
(And still upon the western wild
   Admiring teamsters tell
How Mabel's father cursed his child
   For clearing with a swell.)

BALLAD OF MABEL CLARE II Oil on hardboard 35 cm × 45 cm 1975

"What ails my bird this bridal night?"
   Exclaimed Lord Kawlinee;
"What ails my own this bridal night?
   O Love, confide in me!"
"Oh now," she said, "that I am yaws
   You'll let me weep—I must—
For I've betrayed the people's caws
   And joined the upper crust."

Oh, proudly smiled his lordship then—
  His chimney-pot he floor'd;
"Look up, my love, and smile again,
  For I am not a lord!"
His eye-glass from his eye he tore,
  The dickey from his breast,
And turned and stood his bride before—
  A rouseabout, confess'd!

"Unknown I've loved you long," he said,
  "And I have loved you true—
A-shearing in a neighbour's shed
  I learned to worship you.
I do not care for place or pelf,
  For now, my love, I'm sure
That you will love me for myself
  And not because I'm poor.

"To prove your love I spent my cheque
  To buy this swell rig-out;
So fling your arms about my neck
  For I'm a rouseabout!"
At first she gave a startled cry,
  Then, safe from Care's alarms,
She sighed a soul-subduing sigh
  And sank into his arms.

He pawned the togs, and home he took
  His bride in all her charms;
The proud old cockatoo received
  The pair with open arms.
And long they lived; the faithful bride,
  The lowly rouseabout—
And if she wasn't satisfied
  She never let it out.